AI for All Ages: A Comprehensive Resource for Parents, Seniors, and Students

AI SERIES 2

Erkan YILDIRIM

Table Of Contents

Chapter 1: Understanding Artificial Intelligence   2

Chapter 2: Applications of AI in Everyday Life   7

Chapter 3: Benefits and Risks of AI   13

Chapter 4: How AI is Changing Industries   19

Chapter 5: Getting Started with AI   25

Chapter 6: AI for Parents and Students   30

Chapter 7: AI for Seniors   36

Chapter 8: AI for Entrepreneurs and Small Business
Owners   42

Chapter 9: The Future of AI for All Ages   48

Chapter 10: Conclusion   55

01

Chapter 1:
Understanding Artificial Intelligence

What is Artificial Intelligence?

Artificial Intelligence, often abbreviated as AI, is a term that has been making waves in recent years across various industries. But what exactly is Artificial Intelligence? In simple terms, AI refers to the simulation of human intelligence processes by machines, particularly computer systems. These machines are designed to perform tasks that typically require human intelligence, such as learning, problem-solving, and decision-making. AI is a broad field that encompasses a range of technologies, including machine learning, natural language processing, and robotics.

One of the key characteristics of Artificial Intelligence is its ability to learn from data. Machine learning, a subset of AI, allows machines to analyze large amounts of data and identify patterns or trends within that data. This process enables machines to make predictions or decisions based on the information they have learned. Machine learning algorithms are used in a wide range of applications, from recommendation systems on streaming platforms to self-driving cars.

Another important aspect of Artificial Intelligence is natural language processing (NLP). NLP focuses on enabling machines to understand, interpret, and generate human language. This technology is used in virtual assistants like Siri and Alexa, as well as in chatbots and language translation services. By leveraging NLP, machines can communicate with humans more effectively and efficiently.

Robotics is another area where AI is making significant strides. Robots powered by AI technology can perform a variety of tasks, from manufacturing to healthcare to agriculture. These robots are equipped with sensors and cameras that allow them to perceive their environment and make decisions based on that information. As AI continues to advance, we can expect to see robots playing an increasingly important role in our daily lives.

In conclusion, Artificial Intelligence is a powerful technology that is transforming the way we live and work. From machine learning to natural language processing to robotics, AI is revolutionizing industries and creating new opportunities for innovation. By understanding the basics of AI and its various applications, we can all become better equipped to navigate the increasingly AI-driven world around us.

History of Artificial Intelligence

Artificial Intelligence (AI) has a long and fascinating history that dates back to ancient times. The concept of creating machines that can mimic human intelligence can be traced back to the ancient Greeks and Egyptians who built automata, mechanical devices that could perform simple tasks. However, it wasn't until the 20th century that AI truly began to take shape as a field of study and research.

The term "artificial intelligence" was first coined in 1956 by computer scientist John McCarthy, who organized a conference at Dartmouth College that brought together researchers from various disciplines to explore the possibilities of creating intelligent machines. This event is often considered the birth of AI as a formal academic field. In the decades that followed, researchers made significant advancements in AI, developing algorithms and techniques that allowed computers to perform tasks that were once thought to require human intelligence.

One of the key milestones in the history of AI was the development of expert systems in the 1980s. These systems were designed to mimic the decision-making processes of human experts in specific fields, such as medicine or finance. Expert systems paved the way for the development of other AI technologies, such as natural language processing and machine learning, which have since become integral parts of many modern applications.

In recent years, AI has made significant advancements in areas such as robotics, autonomous vehicles, and healthcare. These developments have raised important ethical and societal questions about the impact of AI on jobs, privacy, and security. As AI continues to evolve and become more integrated into our daily lives, it is crucial for individuals of all ages and backgrounds to understand the history and potential implications of this powerful technology.

In this subchapter, we will explore the history of AI, from its ancient roots to its modern applications. We will examine key milestones and developments in the field, as well as the ethical considerations and challenges that come with the rise of intelligent machines. Whether you are a young adult, parent, senior, student, entrepreneur, or general reader, this chapter will provide you with a comprehensive overview of AI and its relevance in today's world.

Types of Artificial Intelligence

Artificial Intelligence (AI) is a rapidly growing field that has the potential to revolutionize the way we live and work. In order to understand AI better, it is important to explore the different types of AI that exist. In this subchapter, we will delve into the various categories of AI and how they are used in everyday life.

The first type of AI is Narrow AI, also known as Weak AI. This type of AI is designed for specific tasks and functions within a limited context. Examples of Narrow AI include virtual personal assistants like Siri and Alexa, as well as recommendation algorithms used by companies like Netflix and Amazon. Narrow AI is the most common form of AI and is widely used in a variety of industries.

The second type of AI is General AI, also known as Strong AI. This type of AI is designed to have the same intellectual capabilities as a human being, including the ability to understand, learn, and apply knowledge across a wide range of tasks. General AI is still largely theoretical and has not yet been achieved, but researchers are actively working towards this goal.

The third type of AI is Artificial Superintelligence (ASI). ASI refers to AI systems that surpass human intelligence in every way, including creativity, emotional intelligence, and problem-solving abilities. ASI is the ultimate goal of AI research, but it also raises ethical concerns about the potential risks of creating machines that are smarter than humans.

Finally, there is the concept of Hybrid AI, which combines elements of different types of AI to create more advanced and versatile systems. Hybrid AI is becoming increasingly popular as researchers seek to develop AI systems that can perform a wide range of tasks with greater efficiency and accuracy. By blending the strengths of different types of AI, researchers hope to create more powerful and adaptable machines that can benefit society in new and innovative ways.

In conclusion, understanding the different types of AI is essential for anyone interested in the field of artificial intelligence. Whether you are a young adult, parent, senior, student, general reader, entrepreneur, or small business owner, knowing the various categories of AI can help you appreciate the potential of this groundbreaking technology. As AI continues to evolve and expand, it is important to stay informed about the latest developments and trends in order to fully embrace the benefits of this transformative technology.

02

Chapter 2: Applications of AI in Everyday Life

AI in Healthcare

Artificial Intelligence (AI) is rapidly transforming the healthcare industry, revolutionizing the way medical professionals diagnose, treat, and manage patients. In this subchapter, we will explore the various ways AI is being utilized in healthcare and the impact it is having on patients and healthcare providers alike. From advanced diagnostic tools to personalized treatment plans, AI is truly changing the face of modern medicine.

One of the key areas where AI is making a significant impact in healthcare is in diagnostic imaging. AI-powered algorithms are able to analyze medical images such as X-rays, MRIs, and CT scans with incredible accuracy, helping doctors detect diseases and conditions earlier and more effectively than ever before. This not only improves patient outcomes but also helps reduce healthcare costs by minimizing the need for unnecessary tests and procedures.

In addition to diagnostic imaging, AI is also being used to improve patient care through personalized treatment plans. By analyzing vast amounts of patient data, AI algorithms can recommend the most effective treatment options based on a patient's unique medical history, genetic makeup, and other factors. This personalized approach to healthcare not only leads to better outcomes but also helps reduce the risk of adverse reactions to medications and treatments. Another area where AI is making a big impact in healthcare is in administrative tasks. AI-powered tools are being used to streamline processes such as scheduling appointments, processing insurance claims, and managing electronic health records. By automating these tasks, healthcare providers can free up more time to focus on patient care, ultimately improving the overall patient experience.

Overall, AI is revolutionizing the healthcare industry in countless ways, from improving diagnostic accuracy to enhancing patient care and streamlining administrative tasks. As AI continues to advance, it is important for healthcare professionals and patients alike to stay informed about the latest developments in order to take full advantage of the benefits that AI has to offer. Whether you are a young adult, parent, senior, student, entrepreneur, or small business owner, AI in healthcare is a topic that is relevant to us all.

AI in Education

Artificial Intelligence (AI) is revolutionizing the way education is delivered and received. From personalized learning platforms to intelligent tutoring systems, AI is transforming the traditional classroom experience. This subchapter will explore the various ways AI is being used in education and the potential benefits it offers to students of all ages.

One of the key applications of AI in education is personalized learning. By analyzing data on student performance and behavior, AI can tailor educational content to meet the individual needs of each student. This personalized approach helps students learn at their own pace and in a way that is most effective for them, leading to improved academic outcomes.

Another important use of AI in education is in the development of intelligent tutoring systems. These systems use AI algorithms to provide students with real-time feedback and support as they work through educational materials. By offering personalized guidance and assistance, these systems can help students grasp difficult concepts and improve their overall learning experience.

AI can also be used to enhance the assessment process in education. Through the use of AI-powered assessment tools, educators can quickly and accurately evaluate student performance, identify areas for improvement, and provide targeted feedback. This not only saves teachers time but also ensures that students receive the support they need to succeed.

Overall, AI has the potential to revolutionize education by making learning more personalized, engaging, and effective. By leveraging the power of AI technologies, educators can provide students of all ages with the tools and resources they need to thrive in an increasingly digital world. Whether you are a young adult, parent, senior, student, general reader, entrepreneur, or small business owner, AI in education is a topic that is relevant to everyone.

AI in Entertainment

AI has become an integral part of the entertainment industry, revolutionizing the way we consume and interact with media. From personalized recommendations on streaming platforms to creating realistic virtual characters in video games, AI technology is shaping the future of entertainment for audiences of all ages. This subchapter will explore the various ways in which AI is being utilized in the entertainment industry and how it is enhancing the overall experience for consumers.

One of the most prominent applications of AI in entertainment is in the realm of content recommendation. Platforms like Netflix and Spotify use AI algorithms to analyze user data and preferences, in order to suggest personalized content that is likely to be of interest to each individual. This not only helps users discover new movies, TV shows, and music, but also keeps them engaged and coming back for more. By leveraging AI technology, entertainment companies are able to tailor their offerings to the specific tastes and preferences of their audience, ultimately leading to a more satisfying viewing or listening experience.

In addition to content recommendation, AI is also being used in the creation of virtual characters and worlds in video games. Through advanced algorithms and machine learning techniques, game developers are able to generate realistic and dynamic characters that can adapt to the player's actions and decisions. This level of interactivity and immersion enhances the overall gaming experience, making it more engaging and enjoyable for players of all ages. AI-driven game design is pushing the boundaries of what is possible in the world of entertainment, creating new and exciting opportunities for innovation and creativity.

Furthermore, AI technology is also being utilized in the film and television industry to streamline the production process and enhance visual effects. From creating lifelike CGI creatures to automating editing and post-production tasks, AI is helping filmmakers and producers bring their creative visions to life in a more efficient and cost-effective manner. By harnessing the power of AI, entertainment companies are able to deliver high-quality content faster and more affordably, ultimately benefiting both creators and consumers.

Overall, the integration of AI in entertainment is transforming the way we consume and engage with media, offering new and exciting opportunities for audiences of all ages. Whether it's through personalized content recommendations, interactive virtual characters in video games, or advanced visual effects in films and TV shows, AI is enhancing the overall entertainment experience in ways we never thought possible. As technology continues to evolve and improve, the possibilities for AI in entertainment are truly endless, promising a future filled with even more innovative and immersive forms of entertainment for all to enjoy.

03

Chapter 3: Benefits and Risks of AI

Benefits of AI

In today's fast-paced world, artificial intelligence (AI) is becoming increasingly prevalent in our daily lives. From virtual assistants like Siri and Alexa to self-driving cars and personalized recommendations on streaming platforms, AI is revolutionizing the way we live, work, and play. In this subchapter, we will explore the numerous benefits of AI and how it is shaping the future for individuals of all ages and backgrounds.

One of the key benefits of AI is its ability to streamline and automate tasks, saving time and increasing efficiency. For professionals and entrepreneurs, this means being able to focus on more strategic and creative aspects of their work, while mundane tasks are handled by AI-powered tools and software. This not only helps improve productivity but also allows for better decision-making and problem-solving.

For parents and seniors, AI can provide peace of mind and assistance in everyday tasks. From smart home devices that can monitor health and safety to virtual companions that can provide entertainment and companionship, AI offers a wide range of solutions to make life easier and more enjoyable. Additionally, AI can help students and general readers by providing personalized learning experiences, recommending relevant content, and offering real-time feedback to enhance their skills and knowledge.

Entrepreneurs and small business owners can also benefit greatly from AI by gaining valuable insights into customer behavior, market trends, and competitive analysis. By leveraging AI-powered analytics and predictive modeling, businesses can make data-driven decisions that drive growth and success. Furthermore, AI can help identify new opportunities, optimize operations, and create personalized experiences for customers, leading to increased loyalty and revenue.

Overall, AI is a powerful tool that has the potential to transform industries, improve quality of life, and drive innovation. By understanding and embracing the benefits of AI, young adults and professionals, parents, seniors, students, general readers, entrepreneurs, and small business owners can harness its potential to achieve their goals and thrive in the digital age. As AI continues to evolve and become more integrated into our lives, it is essential to stay informed and educated about its capabilities and implications to fully realize its benefits for everyone.

Risks and Ethical Considerations of AI

Artificial Intelligence (AI) has the potential to revolutionize various aspects of our lives, from healthcare to transportation to entertainment. However, along with its benefits, AI also presents risks and ethical considerations that must be carefully considered. In this subchapter, we will delve into some of the key risks associated with AI and the ethical dilemmas that arise from its widespread use.

One of the primary risks of AI is the potential for bias in algorithms. AI systems are only as good as the data they are trained on, and if that data is biased, the AI system will also be biased. This can lead to discrimination against certain groups of people, perpetuating existing inequalities in society. It is crucial for developers to be aware of this risk and take steps to mitigate bias in their AI systems.

Another risk of AI is the potential for job displacement. As AI technology advances, there is a fear that automation will lead to the loss of jobs in many industries. While AI can create new opportunities and increase efficiency, it is important for policymakers to consider the impact on the workforce and implement strategies to support workers who may be displaced by AI.

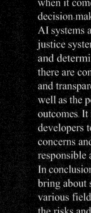

Ethical considerations also come into play when it comes to the use of AI in decision-making processes. For example, AI systems are being used in criminal justice systems to predict recidivism rates and determine sentencing. However, there are concerns about the fairness and transparency of these systems, as well as the potential for bias to influence outcomes. It is vital for policymakers and developers to address these ethical concerns and ensure that AI is used in a responsible and ethical manner.

In conclusion, while AI has the potential to bring about significant advancements in various fields, it is essential to consider the risks and ethical considerations associated with its use. By being aware of these issues and taking proactive measures to address them, we can harness the power of AI in a way that benefits society as a whole. It is up to all of us, from developers to policymakers to the general public, to ensure that AI is used responsibly and ethically for the betterment of all.

Future of AI

The Future of AI is an exciting topic that is constantly evolving and shaping the world around us. As young adults and professionals, it is important to stay informed about the latest advancements in artificial intelligence and how they can impact our lives. From self driving cars to virtual assistants, AI technologies are becoming more integrated into our daily routines, making tasks easier and more efficient.

For parents and seniors, understanding the future of AI can help in preparing the next generation for a world where smart machines are a prominent part of society. It is important to educate children and grandchildren about the potential benefits and challenges that come with AI technology, so they can navigate this rapidly changing landscape with confidence.

Students can also benefit from learning about the future of AI, as it can inspire them to pursue careers in this exciting field. With the demand for AI professionals on the rise, students who have a strong foundation in computer science and mathematics will have numerous opportunities to contribute to groundbreaking advancements in artificial intelligence.

General readers who are curious about AI can also benefit from exploring the future of AI, as it can help them understand how smart machines are changing industries and transforming the way we live and work. By staying informed about the latest trends and developments in AI, readers can better prepare themselves for the future.

Entrepreneurs and small business owners can also leverage AI technologies to streamline operations, improve customer experiences, and gain a competitive edge in their industries. By understanding the potential of AI and how it can be integrated into their businesses, entrepreneurs can take advantage of the countless opportunities that come with embracing smart machines.

04

Chapter 4: How AI is Changing Industries

AI in Finance

Artificial Intelligence (AI) has revolutionized the way we conduct business in many industries, and finance is no exception. In recent years, AI has been increasingly used in the financial sector to improve efficiency, reduce costs, and enhance decision-making processes. From algorithmic trading to fraud detection, AI technologies have the potential to transform the way we manage our finances.

One of the key applications of AI in finance is in algorithmic trading, where computers analyze market data and execute trades at lightning speed. This has the potential to outperform human traders in terms of speed and accuracy, leading to better investment returns. AI algorithms can also be used to predict market trends and identify profitable trading opportunities, giving investors a competitive edge in the volatile world of finance.

Another important use of AI in finance is in fraud detection. By analyzing large volumes of data in real-time, AI systems can identify suspicious patterns and flag potential fraudulent activities before they escalate. This not only helps financial institutions protect their customers' assets but also saves them millions of dollars in losses each year. With the rise of online banking and digital transactions, the need for advanced fraud detection systems powered by AI has never been greater.

In addition to trading and fraud detection, AI is also being used to personalize financial services for consumers. By analyzing customer data and behavior patterns, AI algorithms can recommend personalized investment strategies, insurance plans, and savings goals tailored to individual needs. This level of customization not only improves customer satisfaction but also helps financial institutions retain loyal clients in an increasingly competitive market.

Overall, the integration of AI in finance has the potential to streamline operations, reduce risks, and improve decision-making processes. Whether you're a young adult looking to invest in the stock market, a small business owner in need of financial advice, or a senior planning for retirement, AI technologies can help you make smarter financial decisions. By understanding the impact of AI in finance and embracing its potential, we can all benefit from a more efficient and secure financial future.

AI in Marketing

Artificial Intelligence (AI) has been making waves in the marketing industry, revolutionizing the way businesses connect with their customers. In this subchapter, we will explore the role of AI in marketing and how it is shaping the future of advertising and consumer engagement.

AI in marketing involves the use of advanced algorithms and machine learning to analyze data, predict consumer behavior, and optimize marketing strategies. By leveraging AI technology, businesses can personalize their marketing campaigns, deliver targeted advertisements, and create more engaging content that resonates with their target audience.

One of the key benefits of AI in marketing is its ability to automate repetitive tasks and streamline processes. This not only saves time and resources for businesses but also allows them to focus on more strategic initiatives that drive growth and innovation. AI-powered tools such as chatbots, predictive analytics, and recommendation engines are helping businesses deliver a seamless and personalized customer experience.

For young adults and professionals, understanding the role of AI in marketing is essential for staying competitive in today's digital landscape. By leveraging AI technology, businesses can gain a competitive edge, reach new customers, and drive revenue growth. Whether you are a marketer, entrepreneur, or small business owner, embracing AI in marketing can help you stay ahead of the curve and achieve your business objectives.

In conclusion, AI in marketing is transforming the way businesses connect with their customers and drive growth. By leveraging AI technology, businesses can personalize their marketing campaigns, automate repetitive tasks, and deliver a seamless and personalized customer experience. Whether you are a parent, senior, student, or general reader, understanding the role of AI in marketing is key to staying informed and empowered in today's fast-paced digital world.

AI in Manufacturing

AI in manufacturing is revolutionizing the way products are made and distributed. From the use of robots on the assembly line to predictive maintenance systems, artificial intelligence is playing a key role in increasing efficiency and reducing costs in the manufacturing industry. This subchapter will explore the various ways in which AI is transforming the manufacturing sector and the implications for young adults, professionals, parents, seniors, students, general readers, entrepreneurs, and small business owners.

One of the most significant applications of AI in manufacturing is in predictive maintenance. By using machine learning algorithms to analyze data from sensors on equipment, manufacturers can predict when a machine is likely to fail and perform maintenance before a breakdown occurs. This not only reduces downtime but also extends the lifespan of equipment, saving companies money in the long run.

Another key area where AI is making an impact in manufacturing is in quality control. AI-powered systems can analyze images and data from production lines to identify defects in real-time, allowing manufacturers to catch and address issues before they result in defective products reaching consumers. This not only improves product quality but also enhances customer satisfaction and brand reputation.

AI is also being used in manufacturing to optimize production processes. By analyzing data on factors such as machine performance, energy consumption, and supply chain logistics, AI algorithms can identify opportunities to increase efficiency and reduce waste. This leads to cost savings for manufacturers and a more sustainable approach to production.

For young adults and professionals in the manufacturing industry, understanding how AI is being used in their field is essential for staying competitive in the job market. By familiarizing themselves with AI technologies and learning how to work alongside intelligent machines, they can position themselves as valuable assets to their employers.

Overall, AI in manufacturing is transforming the industry in numerous ways, from predictive maintenance to quality control and process optimization. For parents, seniors, students, general readers, entrepreneurs, and small business owners, staying informed about these advancements in AI can help them make informed decisions about their careers, investments, and purchases. By embracing AI technologies, individuals and businesses can take advantage of the many benefits that intelligent machines have to offer in the manufacturing sector.

05

Chapter 5: Getting Started with AI

Learning AI Basics

In this subchapter titled "Learning AI Basics," we will delve into the foundational concepts of artificial intelligence (AI) that are essential for individuals of all ages and backgrounds to understand. Whether you are a young adult, professional, parent, senior, student, general reader, entrepreneur, or small business owner, grasping the basics of AI is becoming increasingly important in today's technology-driven world.

To begin with, it is crucial to understand what AI actually is. AI refers to the simulation of human intelligence processes by machines, typically computer systems. These processes include learning, reasoning, problem-solving, perception, and language understanding. By mimicking these cognitive functions, AI can perform tasks that typically require human intelligence, such as speech recognition, decision-making, and visual perception.

One of the key components of AI is machine learning, which enables computers to learn and improve from experience without being explicitly programmed. Machine learning algorithms analyze data, identify patterns, and make decisions based on that data. This capability allows AI systems to continuously enhance their performance and accuracy over time, making them increasingly intelligent and efficient.

Another important concept to grasp in AI basics is deep learning, a subset of machine learning that uses artificial neural networks to model and process vast amounts of data. Deep learning is particularly effective for tasks like image and speech recognition, natural language processing, and autonomous driving. Understanding how deep learning works can provide valuable insights into the capabilities and potential applications of AI technology.

In conclusion, learning the basics of AI is crucial for individuals of all ages and backgrounds in today's digital age. By understanding the fundamental concepts of AI, such as machine learning and deep learning, you can gain valuable insights into how AI systems function and their potential applications. Whether you are a young adult, professional, parent, senior, student, general reader, entrepreneur, or small business owner, grasping AI basics will empower you to navigate the increasingly AI-driven world with confidence and understanding.

Resources for Learning AI

In this subchapter, we will explore the various resources available for learning about Artificial Intelligence (AI). Whether you are a young adult looking to expand your knowledge, a parent wanting to introduce your child to this fascinating field, or a senior eager to stay up-to-date with the latest technology, there are resources out there for everyone. From online courses to books and podcasts, the options are endless when it comes to learning about AI.

One of the most popular resources for learning AI is online courses. Platforms like Coursera, Udemy, and edX offer a wide range of courses on AI, machine learning, and deep learning. These courses are designed for individuals of all skill levels, from beginners to advanced users. They typically include video lectures, readings, quizzes, and assignments to help you grasp the concepts and apply them in real-world scenarios.

Books are another valuable resource for learning about AI. There are countless books available on the subject, ranging from introductory guides to in-depth technical manuals. Some popular titles include "Artificial Intelligence: A Guide for Parents and Children," "AI Superpowers: China, Silicon Valley, and the New World Order," and "Machine Learning for Dummies." These books can provide you with a solid foundation in AI principles and help you understand how AI is changing the world around us.

If you prefer to learn on-the-go, podcasts are a convenient way to stay informed about AI. There are numerous podcasts dedicated to discussing the latest developments in AI, machine learning, and robotics. Some popular AI podcasts include "The AI Podcast," "Artificial Intelligence in Industry," and "This Week in Machine Learning & AI." Listening to these podcasts can help you stay up-to-date with the rapidly evolving field of AI and gain insights from industry experts.

In conclusion, there are a plethora of resources available for learning about AI, catering to a wide range of audiences. Whether you prefer online courses, books, podcasts, or a combination of all three, there is something out there for everyone. By taking advantage of these resources, you can deepen your understanding of AI, develop new skills, and stay ahead of the curve in this rapidly advancing field. So go ahead, dive in, and start your AI learning journey today!

AI Tools and Technologies

Artificial Intelligence (AI) is revolutionizing the way we live, work, and interact with technology. In this subchapter, we will explore the various AI tools and technologies that are shaping the future of our world. From voice assistants like Siri and Alexa to self-driving cars and predictive analytics, AI is everywhere and impacting every aspect of our lives.

One of the most popular AI tools that young adults and professionals are utilizing is machine learning. Machine learning algorithms allow computers to learn from data and make decisions without being explicitly programmed. This technology is being used in a wide range of applications, from fraud detection in financial services to personalized recommendations on streaming platforms like Netflix.

For parents and seniors, AI tools like healthcare chatbots and virtual assistants are making it easier to access medical information and support. These tools can provide personalized health advice, remind patients to take their medication, and even schedule appointments with doctors. AI is also being used in the development of wearable devices that can monitor vital signs and alert users to potential health issues.

Students can benefit from AI tools like language translation apps and virtual tutors, which can help them with their homework and language learning. These tools use natural language processing and machine learning to understand and respond to user input, making learning more interactive and engaging. General readers can also take advantage of AI-powered content recommendation engines, which can suggest articles, books, and videos based on their interests and reading habits. Entrepreneurs and small business owners can leverage AI tools like customer relationship management (CRM) software and predictive analytics to improve their operations and grow their businesses. These tools can help companies better understand their customers, predict market trends, and make data-driven decisions. By embracing AI tools and technologies, individuals in all walks of life can enhance their productivity, efficiency, and overall quality of life.

06

Chapter 6: AI for Parents and Students

Using AI for Education

In this subchapter, we will explore how artificial intelligence (AI) is being utilized in the field of education to enhance learning experiences for students of all ages. With the rapid advancements in technology, AI has become an invaluable tool in the education sector, offering personalized learning experiences, improving student engagement, and providing valuable insights for educators.

One of the key ways AI is transforming education is through the use of adaptive learning platforms. These platforms use AI algorithms to analyze students' learning patterns and preferences, enabling them to deliver personalized content and recommendations tailored to each student's individual needs. This not only helps students learn at their own pace but also ensures that they receive the support and resources they need to succeed.

AI-powered virtual tutors are another innovative application of AI in education. These virtual tutors can provide students with immediate feedback, answer questions, and offer personalized study plans based on their performance. By leveraging AI technology, students can receive individualized support and guidance, ultimately improving their academic performance and understanding of complex concepts.

Furthermore, AI is also being used to analyze and interpret large amounts of data to identify trends and patterns that can help educators make informed decisions. By using AI-powered analytics tools, educators can gain valuable insights into student performance, identify areas of improvement, and make data-driven decisions to enhance teaching methods and curriculum development.

Overall, the use of AI in education is revolutionizing the way students learn and educators teach. By harnessing the power of AI technology, schools and educational institutions can provide more personalized and engaging learning experiences, ultimately helping students reach their full potential. As AI continues to evolve and improve, the possibilities for enhancing education through technology are endless.

AI Safety for Children

As artificial intelligence (AI) continues to become more prevalent in our daily lives, it is important to consider the safety implications, especially when it comes to children. AI has the potential to greatly benefit children, enabling personalized learning experiences, interactive toys, and even virtual companions. However, there are also risks associated with AI that parents and caregivers should be aware of to ensure the safety and well-being of their children.

One of the main concerns with AI safety for children is the potential for data privacy and security breaches. Many AI-powered devices and apps collect and store personal information about children, such as their names, ages, and even their locations. This data can be vulnerable to hacking or misuse, putting children at risk of identity theft or other dangers. It is crucial for parents to carefully read privacy policies and settings when allowing their children to use AI devices or apps, and to regularly monitor and limit the data that is being collected.

Another important consideration for AI safety for children is the potential for bias and discrimination in AI algorithms. AI systems are only as good as the data they are trained on, and if that data is biased or incomplete, it can lead to discriminatory outcomes. For example, AI-powered educational tools may inadvertently reinforce stereotypes or provide inaccurate information based on biased data. Parents should be vigilant in monitoring the content and recommendations provided by AI systems to ensure they are appropriate and unbiased for their children. Additionally, there is a growing concern about the potential impact of AI on children's mental and emotional well-being. AI-powered devices and apps can provide constant stimulation and feedback, which may lead to addiction or dependency in children. It is important for parents to set limits on screen time and encourage children to engage in offline activities to promote a healthy balance. Parents should also be aware of the potential for AI systems to manipulate children's emotions or behaviors, and be prepared to address any negative effects that may arise.

In conclusion, while AI has the potential to greatly benefit children in terms of education, entertainment, and companionship, it is important for parents and caregivers to be aware of the safety risks associated with AI. By staying informed, setting boundaries, and monitoring children's interactions with AI devices and apps, parents can help ensure that their children are able to enjoy the benefits of AI while staying safe and protected.

AI Tools for Parents

In today's fast-paced world, parents are constantly looking for ways to make their lives easier and more efficient. With the rise of artificial intelligence (AI) tools, parents now have access to a wide range of resources that can help them navigate the challenges of raising children in the digital age. From educational apps to smart home devices, AI tools for parents are becoming increasingly popular and accessible.

One of the most popular AI tools for parents is the use of educational apps to supplement their child's learning. These apps can provide personalized lessons, track progress, and offer feedback to help children learn at their own pace. With AI technology, parents can feel confident that their child is receiving a quality education, even outside of the classroom.

In addition to educational apps, AI-powered smart home devices are also revolutionizing the way parents manage their households. From smart thermostats that adjust to your family's schedule to AI-powered virtual assistants that can help with scheduling and organization, these devices can help parents stay on top of their busy lives. With the help of AI tools, parents can streamline their daily routines and spend more quality time with their children.

For parents of seniors, AI tools can also offer peace of mind and assistance in caring for their loved ones. From remote monitoring devices that can track vital signs to AI-powered medication reminders, these tools can help seniors maintain their independence and stay safe at home. With the use of AI technology, parents can feel confident that their elderly family members are receiving the care and attention they need.

Overall, AI tools for parents offer a wide range of benefits and opportunities to enhance the parenting experience. Whether it's using educational apps to support learning, smart home devices to streamline household management, or remote monitoring tools for senior care, AI technology is changing the way parents navigate the challenges of raising children in the 21st century. By embracing these tools, parents can feel empowered and confident in their ability to provide a safe and nurturing environment for their children.

07

Chapter 7: AI for Seniors

AI for Healthcare Monitoring

AI for healthcare monitoring is revolutionizing the way we track and manage our health. With the advancement of artificial intelligence technology, healthcare professionals are able to monitor patients remotely, predict potential health issues, and provide personalized care like never before. This subchapter explores the various applications of AI in healthcare monitoring and how it is benefiting individuals of all ages.

One of the key benefits of AI in healthcare monitoring is the ability to collect and analyze vast amounts of data in real-time. By utilizing AI algorithms, healthcare providers can track vital signs, detect anomalies, and predict potential health risks before they escalate. This proactive approach to monitoring allows for early intervention and personalized treatment plans, ultimately improving patient outcomes and reducing healthcare costs.

For young adults and professionals, AI healthcare monitoring offers convenience and peace of mind. With wearable devices and smartphone apps powered by AI, individuals can track their own health metrics, receive personalized recommendations, and even consult with healthcare providers remotely. This level of accessibility and convenience empowers individuals to take control of their health and make informed decisions about their well-being.

Parents and seniors also benefit greatly from AI healthcare monitoring. For parents, AI technology provides a way to monitor their children's health remotely, track medication schedules, and receive alerts for potential health issues. For seniors, AI-powered devices can help them manage chronic conditions, stay connected to caregivers, and maintain their independence for longer. These advancements in healthcare monitoring are transforming the way families care for their loved ones and ensuring peace of mind for all involved.

Students, general readers, entrepreneurs, and small business owners can also benefit from AI healthcare monitoring by staying informed about the latest advancements in the field. Whether they are interested in pursuing a career in healthcare technology, developing new AI-powered devices, or simply staying up-to-date on the latest trends, understanding the impact of AI in healthcare monitoring is essential. By embracing AI technology and its potential to improve healthcare outcomes for everyone, we can create a healthier and more connected world for all ages.

AI for Independent Living

In today's rapidly advancing technological landscape, artificial intelligence (AI) has emerged as a powerful tool for promoting independent living among individuals of all ages. From smart home devices that can assist with daily tasks to virtual health assistants that can monitor health metrics, AI is revolutionizing the way we approach independent living. This subchapter will explore the various ways in which AI can be used to support individuals in maintaining their independence and quality of life.

One of the key benefits of AI for independent living is the ability to automate routine tasks and provide personalized assistance. For young adults and professionals juggling busy schedules, AI-powered personal assistants can help manage calendars, schedule appointments, and even anticipate needs based on past behavior. For seniors looking to age in place, smart home devices equipped with AI technology can provide reminders for medication, monitor activity levels, and even detect potential safety hazards in the home.

Students can also benefit from AI tools that can assist with studying, time management, and organization. AI-powered tutoring programs can provide personalized feedback and guidance, while smart study planners can help students stay on track with assignments and deadlines. By leveraging AI technology, students can optimize their learning experience and achieve academic success.

General readers interested in AI for independent living can explore the various applications of AI in healthcare, such as virtual health assistants that can provide medical advice, monitor chronic conditions, and even detect early warning signs of health issues. Entrepreneurs and small business owners can also leverage AI to streamline operations, improve customer service, and optimize decision-making processes. By embracing AI technology, individuals in all walks of life can enhance their independence and well-being. In conclusion, AI for independent living offers a wide range of benefits for individuals of all ages and backgrounds. Whether you are a young adult looking to boost productivity, a senior seeking to age in place, a student aiming for academic success, or an entrepreneur striving for business growth, AI has the potential to transform the way you live and work. By staying informed about the latest AI advancements and exploring how they can be integrated into your daily life, you can harness the power of AI to support your goals and enhance your overall quality of life.

AI Assistants for Seniors

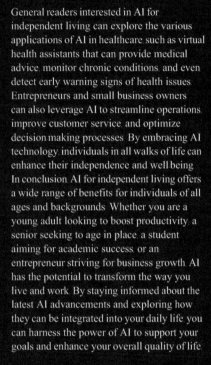

As technology continues to advance, AI assistants are becoming increasingly popular among seniors looking for ways to simplify their daily lives. AI assistants, such as Amazon's Alexa and Google Assistant, offer a wide range of features that can help seniors with tasks ranging from setting reminders to controlling smart home devices. These AI assistants are designed to be user-friendly and intuitive, making them an ideal tool for seniors who may not be as tech-savvy as younger generations.

One of the key benefits of AI assistants for seniors is their ability to provide companionship and support. Loneliness and isolation are common issues among seniors, especially those who live alone or have limited mobility. AI assistants can help alleviate these feelings by providing conversation, playing music, and even telling jokes. This can help seniors feel less alone and more connected to the world around them.

In addition to providing companionship, AI assistants can also help seniors stay organized and on top of their daily tasks. For example, they can set reminders for medication, appointments, and other important events. They can also help with tasks like making grocery lists, ordering food delivery, and managing finances. This can be particularly useful for seniors who may struggle with memory issues or have difficulty keeping track of multiple tasks at once.

Furthermore, AI assistants can help seniors stay safe and independent in their own homes. They can be programmed to send alerts in case of emergencies, such as a fall or sudden illness. They can also control smart home devices, such as thermostats and lighting, to make the home environment more comfortable and accessible for seniors with limited mobility. This can give both seniors and their loved ones peace of mind knowing that help is always just a voice command away.

Overall, AI assistants have the potential to greatly improve the quality of life for seniors by providing companionship, support, and assistance with daily tasks. As technology continues to evolve, it is important for seniors, their families, and caregivers to explore the many ways in which AI assistants can be integrated into their daily routines. By embracing these smart technologies, seniors can enjoy greater independence, safety, and peace of mind in their golden years.

08

Chapter 8: AI for Entrepreneurs and Small Business Owners

Using AI for Business Growth

In today's rapidly evolving business landscape, the use of artificial intelligence (AI) has become increasingly prevalent across industries. From streamlining operations to improving customer experiences, AI has proven to be a powerful tool for driving business growth. In this subchapter, we will explore how young adults, professionals, parents, seniors, students, general readers, entrepreneurs, and small business owners can leverage AI to unlock new opportunities and achieve success. One of the key ways in which AI can contribute to business growth is through automation. By automating repetitive tasks and processes, businesses can free up valuable time and resources that can be redirected towards more strategic initiatives. For young adults and professionals looking to streamline their workflow, AI-powered tools such as chatbots and virtual assistants can help increase efficiency and productivity.

For parents and seniors, AI can offer a range of benefits, from personalized recommendations to improved healthcare services. By harnessing the power of AI-driven algorithms, businesses can better understand their customers' preferences and behavior, allowing them to tailor their products and services to meet their needs more effectively. This level of personalized engagement can lead to increased customer satisfaction and loyalty, ultimately driving business growth.

Students can also benefit from AI in their academic and professional pursuits. By utilizing AI-powered learning platforms and tools, students can access personalized study plans, feedback, and resources that can help them achieve their academic goals. Additionally, AI can help students develop essential skills such as critical thinking, problem-solving, and data analysis, which are increasingly in demand in today's job market.

Entrepreneurs and small business owners can leverage AI to gain a competitive edge in their respective industries. Whether it's optimizing supply chain management, enhancing marketing strategies, or improving customer service, AI can help businesses of all sizes achieve greater efficiency and profitability. By embracing AI technologies, entrepreneurs can unlock new growth opportunities and stay ahead of the curve in an increasingly digital world.

AI Marketing Strategies

In today's digital age, AI marketing strategies have become essential for businesses looking to stay competitive in the market. From personalized recommendations to chatbots, artificial intelligence is revolutionizing the way companies engage with their customers. In this subchapter, we will explore the various AI marketing strategies that young adults, professionals, parents, seniors, students, general readers, entrepreneurs, and small business owners can leverage to enhance their marketing efforts.

One of the most popular AI marketing strategies is using machine learning algorithms to analyze customer data and create personalized marketing campaigns. By understanding customer behavior and preferences, businesses can tailor their messages to resonate with their target audience. This level of personalization not only increases engagement but also drives higher conversion rates.

Another effective AI marketing strategy is the use of chatbots to provide instant customer support. Chatbots can answer frequently asked questions, assist with product recommendations, and even process orders without the need for human intervention. This not only improves customer satisfaction but also frees up employees to focus on more strategic tasks.

AI-powered content creation is also gaining popularity among businesses looking to streamline their marketing efforts. With natural language processing capabilities, AI can generate high-quality content, including blog posts, social media updates, and email newsletters. This allows businesses to maintain a consistent presence online while saving time and resources.

Lastly, predictive analytics is a powerful AI marketing strategy that enables businesses to forecast customer behavior and trends. By analyzing historical data and identifying patterns, businesses can make data-driven decisions that drive business growth. Whether it's predicting customer churn or optimizing pricing strategies, predictive analytics can give businesses a competitive edge in the market.

In conclusion, AI marketing strategies are transforming the way businesses connect with their customers and drive revenue. By leveraging machine learning algorithms, chatbots, content creation tools, and predictive analytics, young adults, professionals, parents, seniors, students, general readers, entrepreneurs, and small business owners can unlock new opportunities for growth and success in the digital age.

AI Customer Service Solutions

In today's fast-paced world, businesses are constantly looking for ways to improve their customer service experience. One solution that has gained popularity in recent years is AI customer service solutions. These innovative tools use artificial intelligence to provide quick and efficient assistance to customers, helping businesses save time and money while also improving customer satisfaction.

AI customer service solutions come in many forms, from chatbots that can answer common questions to sophisticated virtual assistants that can handle complex issues. These tools use natural language processing and machine learning algorithms to understand and respond to customer inquiries, providing a personalized and efficient experience for users.

For young adults and professionals, AI customer service solutions offer a convenient way to get the help they need without having to wait on hold or navigate through complex phone trees. These tools can provide instant responses to common questions, freeing up valuable time for busy individuals to focus on more important tasks.

Parents and seniors can also benefit from AI customer service solutions, as they provide a user-friendly interface that is easy to navigate and understand. These tools can help older adults access information and support services more easily, improving their overall quality of life and independence.

Students, general readers, entrepreneurs, and small business owners can all benefit from AI customer service solutions as well. These tools can help students access educational resources, provide entrepreneurs with valuable customer insights, and assist small business owners in providing top-notch customer service without breaking the bank. Overall, AI customer service solutions are a valuable resource for individuals of all ages and backgrounds, offering a convenient and efficient way to access the help and support they need.

09

Chapter 9: The Future of AI for All Ages

Trends in AI Development

In recent years, the field of artificial intelligence (AI) has experienced rapid growth and development, leading to a number of exciting trends that are shaping the future of this technology. One trend that is particularly noteworthy is the increasing focus on machine learning, a branch of AI that involves training machines to learn from data and improve their performance over time. This has led to significant advancements in areas such as natural language processing, image recognition, and autonomous driving. Another important trend in AI development is the growing emphasis on ethics and responsible AI. As AI systems become more powerful and autonomous, there is a growing recognition of the need to ensure that these systems are developed and used in a way that is ethical and respects human rights. This has led to the emergence of new frameworks and guidelines for the ethical development and deployment of AI, as well as increased scrutiny of AI applications in areas such as healthcare, law enforcement, and finance.

One trend that is particularly exciting for young adults and professionals is the increasing democratization of AI technology. Thanks to advances in cloud computing and open source software, AI tools and platforms are becoming more accessible to a wider range of users, allowing individuals and organizations to leverage the power of AI in new and innovative ways. This trend is opening up new opportunities for entrepreneurs and small business owners to incorporate AI into their products and services, helping them to stay competitive in an increasingly digital world.

Another trend that is of interest to parents and students is the growing use of AI in education. AI technologies are being used to personalize learning experiences, provide real time feedback to students, and automate administrative tasks for teachers. This has the potential to revolutionize the way that education is delivered and make learning more engaging and effective for students of all ages. By staying informed about the latest trends in AI development, parents and students can better understand how AI is shaping the future of education and prepare themselves for success in a rapidly changing world.

Overall, the field of AI is constantly evolving, with new trends and developments emerging on a regular basis. By staying informed about these trends, young adults and professionals, parents, seniors, students, general readers, entrepreneurs, and small business owners can better understand the potential impact of AI on their lives and industries. Whether you are interested in using AI to improve your business, enhance your education, or simply stay informed about the latest advancements in technology, there has never been a better time to explore the exciting world of artificial intelligence.

AI Career Opportunities

Artificial Intelligence (AI) is revolutionizing industries across the globe, creating a wide range of career opportunities for individuals of all ages and backgrounds. As young adults and professionals, it is important to understand the vast potential of AI in today's job market. From data science to machine learning engineering, there are numerous pathways to explore within the field of AI. By gaining a solid understanding of AI principles and technologies, you can position yourself for success in this rapidly growing field.

For parents and seniors, AI career opportunities present an exciting way to stay relevant in an ever-changing job market. Whether you are looking to upskill in your current profession or transition into a new field, AI offers a wealth of possibilities. By taking advantage of online courses, workshops, and certifications, you can equip yourself with the knowledge and skills needed to thrive in an AI-driven world. From healthcare to finance, AI is reshaping the way we work and interact with technology, offering new avenues for career growth and development.

Students are also well-positioned to capitalize on the career opportunities offered by AI. By pursuing degrees in computer science, data analytics, or AI-specific fields, students can gain a competitive edge in the job market. Internships, research projects, and networking events can also help students build valuable connections and experience within the AI industry. By staying informed about the latest trends and developments in AI, students can position themselves for success in a rapidly evolving job market.

For general readers, entrepreneurs, and small business owners, AI career opportunities provide a unique chance to innovate and grow their businesses. By leveraging AI technologies such as chatbots, recommendation engines, and predictive analytics, businesses can gain a competitive edge in their respective industries. From automating routine tasks to personalizing customer experiences, AI offers a wide range of benefits for businesses of all sizes. By investing in AI training and resources, entrepreneurs and small business owners can unlock new opportunities for growth and success.

In conclusion, AI career opportunities are abundant and diverse, offering something for everyone interested in this exciting field. Whether you are a young adult looking to launch your career, a parent or senior seeking to upskill, a student pursuing a degree, or an entrepreneur looking to innovate, AI has something to offer. By staying informed, seeking out training and educational opportunities, and networking with industry professionals, you can position yourself for success in the dynamic world of AI. Embrace the future of work with AI and unlock your full potential in this rapidly evolving field.

AI for Social Good

Artificial Intelligence (AI) has the potential to bring about significant positive change in society, particularly in the realm of social good. In this subchapter, we will explore how AI can be used to address pressing social issues and make a positive impact on communities around the world. From healthcare to education to environmental conservation, AI has the power to revolutionize the way we approach some of the most critical challenges facing humanity today.

One area where AI is already making a significant impact is in healthcare. AI-powered tools can help doctors diagnose diseases more accurately and quickly, leading to better outcomes for patients. Additionally, AI can be used to analyze large amounts of medical data to identify trends and patterns that can help researchers develop new treatments and cures for diseases. By harnessing the power of AI, we can improve healthcare outcomes for people around the world and save lives in the process.

Education is another area where AI has the potential to make a positive impact. AI-powered tutoring systems can provide personalized learning experiences for students, helping them to master difficult concepts and improve their academic performance. Additionally, AI can be used to automate administrative tasks in schools, freeing up teachers to focus more on teaching and interacting with students. By leveraging AI in education, we can create a more equitable and effective learning environment for students of all ages and backgrounds.

Environmental conservation is another area where AI can play a crucial role in driving positive change. AI-powered sensors can monitor environmental conditions in real time, allowing researchers to track changes in ecosystems and respond quickly to environmental threats. Additionally, AI can be used to optimize energy consumption and reduce waste, helping to mitigate the impact of human activity on the planet. By harnessing the power of AI for environmental conservation, we can work towards a more sustainable and environmentally conscious future for all.

In conclusion, AI has the potential to revolutionize the way we address social issues and make a positive impact on communities around the world. From healthcare to education to environmental conservation, AI-powered tools and technologies can help us tackle some of the most pressing challenges facing humanity today. By embracing AI for social good, we can create a more equitable, sustainable, and prosperous future for all.

10

Chapter 10:
Conclusion

Recap of Key Points

In this subchapter, we will recap some of the key points discussed throughout the book "AI for All Ages: A Comprehensive Resource for Parents, Seniors, and Students." Whether you are a young adult, professional, parent, senior, student, general reader, entrepreneur, or small business owner, understanding the basics of artificial intelligence (AI) is essential in today's rapidly evolving technological landscape.

One of the fundamental concepts we covered is the definition of AI and its various applications in everyday life. AI refers to the simulation of human intelligence processes by machines, including learning, reasoning, and self-correction. From virtual assistants like Siri and Alexa to self-driving cars and personalized recommendations on streaming platforms, AI is integrated into numerous aspects of our daily routines.

We also delved into the ethical considerations surrounding AI, including issues related to bias, privacy, and job displacement. As AI systems become more sophisticated, it is crucial to ensure that they are developed and deployed responsibly to minimize negative impacts on society. This requires thoughtful regulation, transparency, and accountability from both developers and users.

Furthermore, we explored the potential benefits of AI for individuals and businesses, such as increased efficiency, improved decision-making, and enhanced customer experiences. By leveraging AI tools and technologies, entrepreneurs and small business owners can streamline operations, gain insights into market trends, and deliver personalized products and services to their target audiences.

Lastly, we highlighted the importance of lifelong learning and staying informed about the latest advancements in AI. As AI continues to evolve at a rapid pace, it is essential for individuals of all ages and backgrounds to keep up with new developments and acquire the skills needed to thrive in an AI-driven world. By embracing AI for everyone, we can unlock its full potential and create a more inclusive and equitable future for all.

Final Thoughts on AI for All Ages

In conclusion, it is evident that AI has the potential to revolutionize the way we live, work, and interact with technology. As we have explored throughout this book, AI is not just for tech-savvy professionals or young students - it is for everyone. From parents looking to simplify their daily tasks to seniors seeking assistance with healthcare, AI can benefit individuals of all ages and backgrounds.

For young adults and professionals, embracing AI can open up new opportunities for career growth and innovation. By gaining a deeper understanding of AI and its applications, you can stay ahead of the curve in a rapidly evolving technological landscape. Whether you work in healthcare, finance, or education, AI has the potential to streamline processes, improve efficiency, and drive meaningful change in your industry.

Parents can also benefit from incorporating AI into their daily routines. From smart home devices that simplify household tasks to educational apps that support children's learning, AI can help parents manage their busy lives more effectively. By leveraging AI-powered tools and resources, parents can create a more efficient and engaging environment for their families.

Seniors, too, can find value in AI technologies that support their health and well-being. From virtual assistants that provide reminders and medication alerts to wearable devices that track vital signs, AI can help seniors age in place more comfortably and independently. By embracing AI solutions tailored to their needs, seniors can maintain their quality of life and stay connected to their communities.

In conclusion. AI for all ages is a comprehensive resource that empowers readers to harness the power of AI in their daily lives. Whether you are a young adult seeking career opportunities, a parent looking to simplify your routine, a senior in need of support or a student eager to learn more about AI, this book is designed to help you navigate the world of artificial intelligence with confidence and ease Embrace the possibilities of AI and discover how smart machines can enhance your life in ways you never thought possible

AI for Everyone: Your No-Brainer Guide to Super Smart Machines

Ditch Sci-Fi, AI's Here! Ever wonder how your phone "reads" your mind (song suggestions, anyone?)? It's AI magic, and it's real! This beginner-friendly guide breaks down complex AI concepts with fun pictures and real-life examples. Inside you'll discover: AI Made Simple: No confusing jargon! You'll learn how AI works, from music picks to faster routes.

AI in Action: See how AI impacts you daily, from shopping to voice assistants (Alexa, Siri, anyone?). The Future of AI: Buckle up! Imagine talking fridges and self-driving cars! We explore the amazing possibilities. But wait! This book also tackles important questions about AI's limitations and ethical considerations. Curious young adult, concerned parent, or just tech-savvy?

This book is for YOU! Unlock the fascinating world of AI and embrace the future with confidence!